The Platypus

What is it?

Jo Brice

Illustrated by Gregory Rogers

PUFFIN BOOKS

To Peter and Janette, who are wild about wildlife. – J. B.
For Narelle, Greg and Rob. – G. R.

Puffin Books
Penguin Books Australia Ltd
487 Maroondah Highway, PO Box 257
Ringwood, Victoria 3134, Australia
Penguin Books Ltd
Harmondsworth, Middlesex, England
Penguin Putnam Inc.
375 Hudson Street, New York, New York 10014, USA
Penguin Books Canada Limited
10 Alcorn Avenue, Toronto, Ontario, Canada, M4V 3B2
Penguin Books (N.Z.) Ltd
Cnr Rosedale and Airborne Roads, Albany, Auckland, New Zealand
Penguin Books (South Africa) (Pty) Ltd
5 Watkins Street, Denver Ext 4, 2094, South Africa
Penguin Books India (P) Ltd
11, Community Centre, Panchsheel Park, New Delhi –110 017, India

First published in Puffin, 2000

10 9 8 7 6 5 4 3 2 1

Text copyright © Jo Brice, 2000
Illustrations copyright © Gregory Rogers, 2000

All rights reserved. Without limiting the rights under copyright
reserved above, no part of this publication may be reproduced,
stored in or introduced into a retrieval system, or transmitted,
in any form or by any means (electronic, mechanical, photocopying,
recording or otherwise), without the prior written permission
of both the copyright owner and the above publisher of this book.

Designed by John Canty, Penguin Design Studio
Typeset in Bembo
Made and printed by Bookbuilders, Hong Kong

National Library of Australia
Cataloguing-in-Publication data:

Brice, Jo
The Platypus: what is it?

Includes index
ISBN 0 14 130692 0

1. Platypus – Juvenile literature I. Rogers, Gregory II. Title

Contents

Introduction *iv*

Creation of Mullangong *1*

What does a platypus look like? *2*

Where does a platypus live? *8*

How does a platypus eat? *11*

How does a platypus breed? *15*

What dangers does a platypus face? *25*

What can people do to help? *28*

Further reading *28*

Index *29*

Introduction

The platypus is an incredible animal. It is a mammal which can lay eggs, and swim underwater as well as any seal or otter. It has a bill like a duck's beak, a flat tail, webs on its front feet, and an amazing radar system for finding food.

The platypus has survived for a very long time. Its ancestor, the *Obdurondon insignis*, was on the Earth one hundred and twenty million years ago. Scientists in London, who saw the first platypus specimen in 1798, thought that it was a hoax. Some thought that it was a joke. Others thought that it had been glued together. But the Australian Aborigines have known this animal for thousands of years.

Creation of Mullangong

A long time ago, a family of ducks lived in a billabong, near a big river. The ducks never left the billabong because they were afraid of Mullaka, the water-rat. One day, a duck wandered off downstream. She swam until she was exhausted, and sat on the riverbank to rest.

Mullaka, the water-rat, came out of his burrow and dragged her underground, where she became his wife. The duck stayed with him for a long time. One day, Mullaka went on a trip. While he was away, the duck escaped and went back to her family. In time, she made her nest and sat on her eggs. She was proud of her two chicks, until she saw how different they were from the other ducklings.

Her chicks had four legs instead of two, fur instead of feathers, webs on their feet and very peculiar beaks. The chicks could swim, but they couldn't fly. The other ducks and drakes laughed at them. So, one day, the duck herded her chicks back to the river, where they made their nests in burrows.

They were the first platypuses in the world.

The name 'platypus' comes from the Greek, which means 'flat foot'.

What does a platypus look like?

Fur

Platypus fur is amazingly soft, and the most waterproof fur that is known.

The fur of a platypus insulates its body just as a wetsuit does for a human. It traps bubbles of air in the fur, which help to keep the platypus warm and almost dry as it swims in cold water.

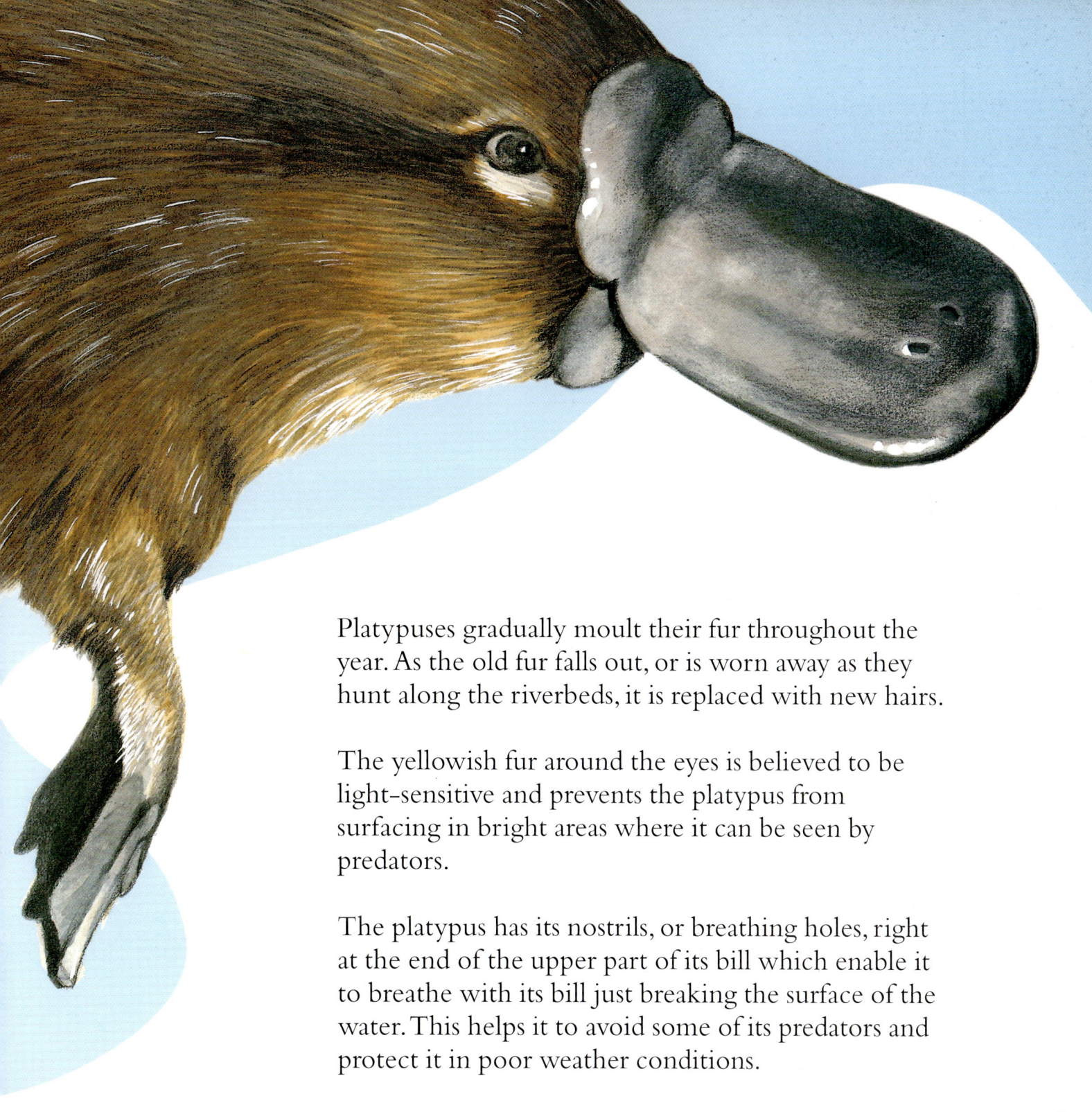

Platypuses gradually moult their fur throughout the year. As the old fur falls out, or is worn away as they hunt along the riverbeds, it is replaced with new hairs.

The yellowish fur around the eyes is believed to be light-sensitive and prevents the platypus from surfacing in bright areas where it can be seen by predators.

The platypus has its nostrils, or breathing holes, right at the end of the upper part of its bill which enable it to breathe with its bill just breaking the surface of the water. This helps it to avoid some of its predators and protect it in poor weather conditions.

Spurs

All platypuses are born with a spur, which looks like a shark's tooth, on the inside of the upper part of their hind legs. The females shed their spurs during their first year but in the male it continues to develop.

Through this spur runs a canal attached to a gland which produces venom. If the platypus has to defend itself, it will sink its spurs and shoot venom into the wound. This venom is strong enough to kill a dog and is extremely painful to humans.

When the male platypus grasps his enemy, both spurs are thrust together into the victim. The harder the victim tries to escape, the harder the platypus thrusts both his spurs and the more venom is injected.

Platypuses are very shy creatures. They will always dive underwater, and race to their burrows when they are frightened or disturbed by even small noises. The males will attack only if they are cornered and cannot escape.

Legs

Platypuses have short legs, which are splayed or turned outwards, like those of crocodiles. But instead of scaly skin, like reptiles, they have fur which reaches right down to their toes.

They swim by using their front feet as paddles. To help them, they have a large floppy web on each front foot. Unlike other creatures, platypuses can roll up the webs on their front feet to keep them out of the way when they are digging their burrows.

The hind feet are only partly webbed.
The webs are fixed and cannot be moved.
But as they use their hind feet mainly as
rudders and brakes, it doesn't really matter.

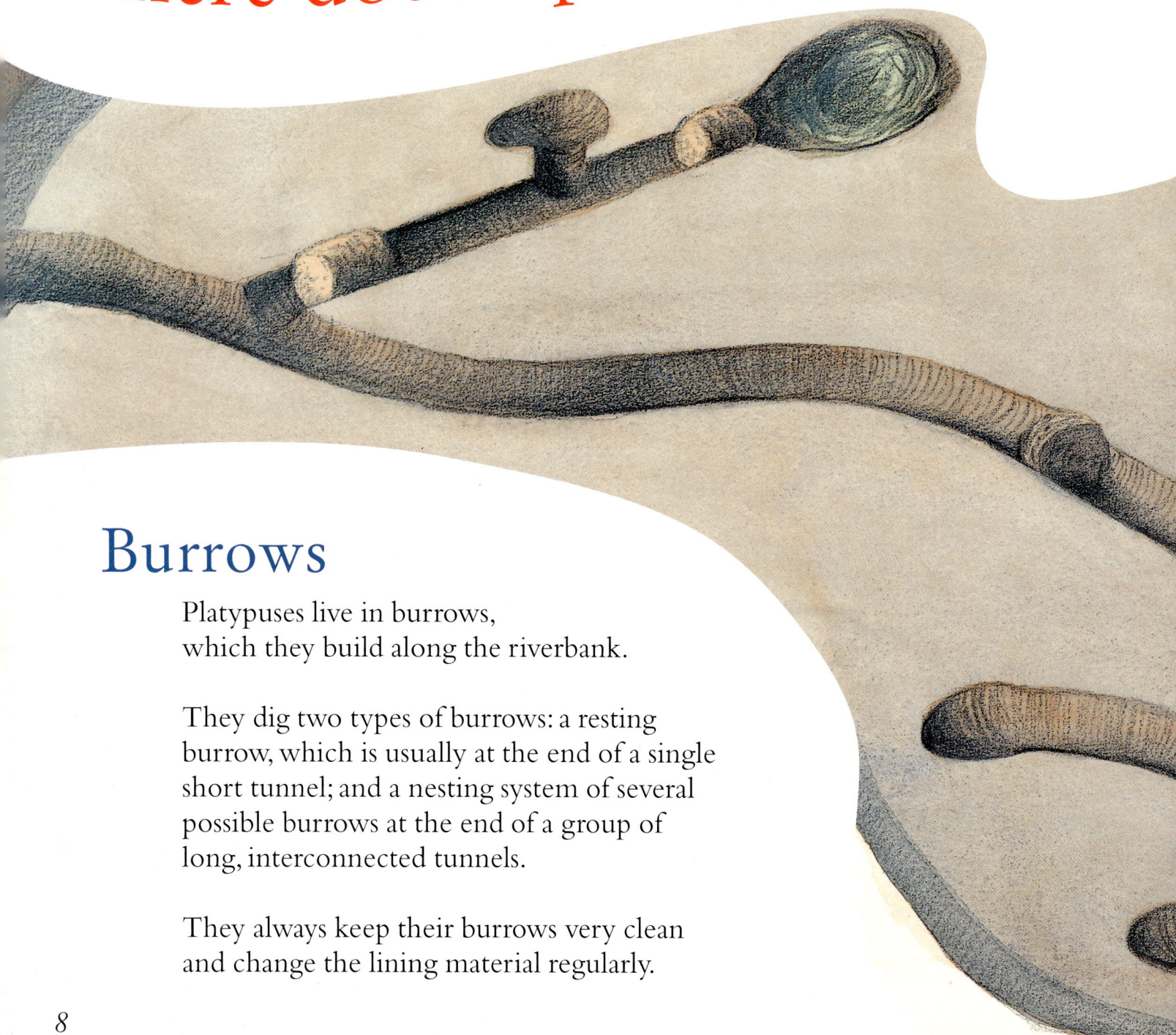

Where does a platypus live?

Burrows

Platypuses live in burrows, which they build along the riverbank.

They dig two types of burrows: a resting burrow, which is usually at the end of a single short tunnel; and a nesting system of several possible burrows at the end of a group of long, interconnected tunnels.

They always keep their burrows very clean and change the lining material regularly.

To get into their burrows, they pull away the doors of mud and leaves. They shake themselves like dogs to get rid of any water and bits of debris on their fur. Then they squeeze through the tight entrance and travel along the narrow tunnels.

Sometimes platypuses share a resting burrow and they may dig several of these along the stretch of the riverbank where they live. But they often live alone, with only the mother and her babies in a nesting burrow.

Hibernation

In the winter, platypuses semi-hibernate. They remain in their burrows for long periods of time, but they wake up and come out for quick hunting expeditions, or to clean out their nests.

As soon as it warms up in spring, they start hunting and playing again.

How does a platypus eat?

Food

Platypuses hunt for their food in rivers and creeks.

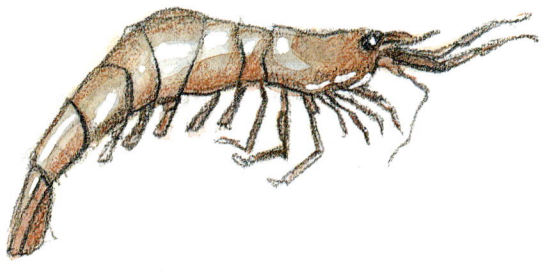

Their favourite food is the freshwater crayfish (yabbies) which they find among the pebbles and dead logs lying on the riverbed. They hold the crayfish with their two front feet as they grind bits of it inside their bills, and then they try to catch the leftovers before they sink.

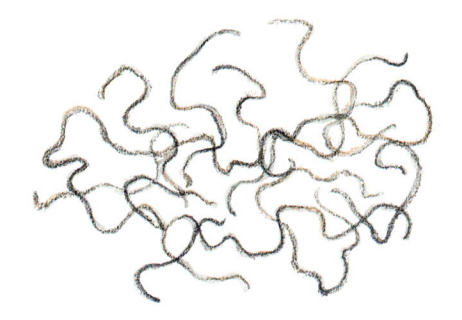

If there are no crayfish, platypuses eat insect larvae, other small water creatures and small frogs.

Teeth

Platypuses are born with full sets of upper and lower teeth, but they lose these after they are a year old. Instead, they grow an upper and lower hard pad, or plate, which they use to grind up their food.

They often collect and use grit from the riverbed to help their grinding plates break up their food. Unlike other mammals which lose their teeth, platypuses just grow more plates after each set wears out.

The serrations on both sides of the hard pad are believed to help with the sorting of bits of food from grit.

Bills

Platypuses can keep their eyes open under water, but it is their bills which help them to find food. The black rubbery bill is full of very small pores, which pick up the tiny electrical waves given off by even the tiniest creature. It works like radar and lets them find something to eat even when the water is muddy.

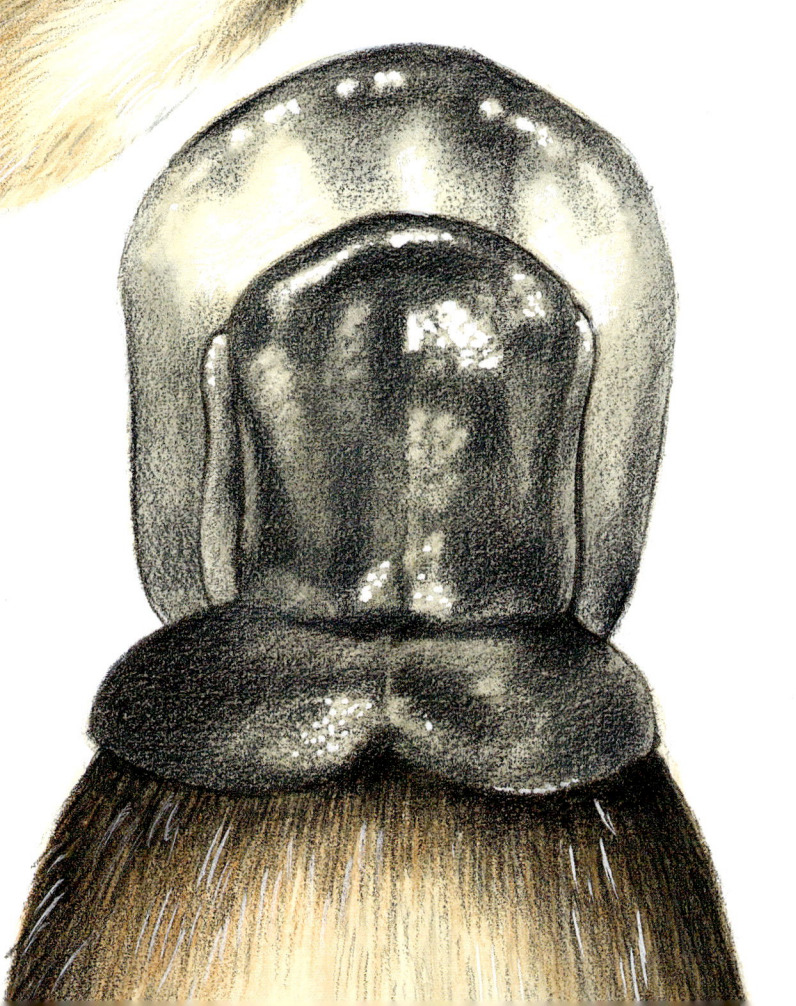

Platypuses have to eat, at least, half their body
weight every twenty-four hours just to grow,
keep themselves warm in cold water,
and hunt for food.

When platypuses are
well-fed, they are very active.
Their fur is sleek and shiny, and their tails are
thick and firm.

How does a platypus breed?

Mating

Mating season for the platypus is during late spring or early summer, when the weather and water are warmer. When they find a mate, they get to know each other by playing and dancing together.

The male chases the female around in the water until he catches her tail in his bill, then they circle round and round in a courtship dance.

The male mates with the female by holding her steady with his front claws and, after pushing her tail out of the way, he tucks his tail up under her belly.

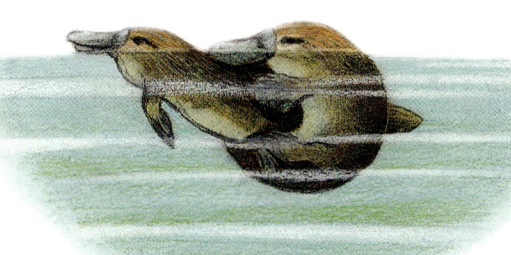

Nesting

After mating, the female is busier than ever. She prepares her nest in the burrow farthest from the entrance to her nesting burrow system. For many days she either hunts, or collects bundles of grass and leaf litter, which she drags into her burrow to make a warm and comfortable lining for the nest.

She gathers her bundles of lining material with her front feet, and pushes each bundle under her where it is held firmly by her back feet and tail.

About twenty days after mating, the female lays one to three eggs, with two being the most common.

Eggs

Platypus eggs are soft-shelled and leathery, similar to those of the turtle, but not nearly so big. They are about the size of a large grape and very delicate. The eggs must be kept moist all the time or they will become brittle and crack open before the babies are ready.

The mother collects a little water on her fur and shakes it over the eggs every now and then. She also changes the nest lining with fresh wet leaves when
the old ones dry out.

Platypuses don't sit on their eggs
to keep them warm – the eggs sit
on them! The mother lies on her back and,
in a semi-sitting position, pushes the eggs
into the fur on her belly. She holds them in
place and keeps them warm by curling her
tail upwards.

Birth

After ten days or so the baby platypuses emerge from their eggs. They do this by breaking through the leathery shells with their egg-tooth, which drops out within a day or two.

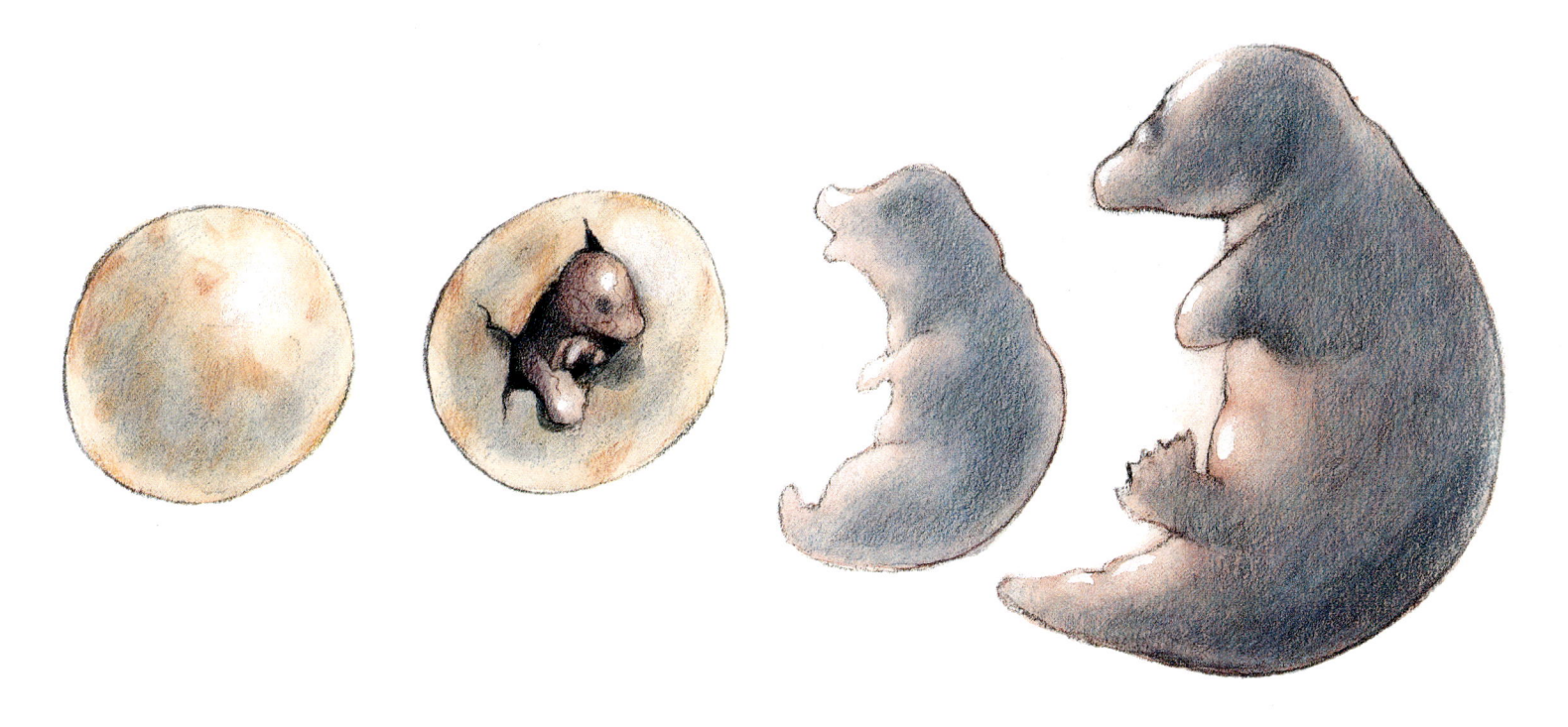

Baby platypuses are tiny – about 1.5 centimetres long. That's almost the size of the end of your thumb. Their eyes stay shut for ten weeks and they don't leave the nest until they are about sixteen weeks old.

Platypuses feed their babies on milk, but the mothers do not have breasts or nipples. Instead, they have milk glands under the skin of their bellies which are covered with rough fur. To get milk, the babies have to nuzzle these two patches of fur until milk seeps out and they can lap it up.

The milk is very rich and contains plenty of iron. If the mother is healthy, the milk has a high level of fat in it, which helps the babies to grow quickly.

Soon, the babies are about half the size of their mother and ready to emerge from the nest.

The babies play in the water
and dive after their mother as she
teaches them to hunt for their own food.
They will need their mother's help for at
least a year and will not be fully grown until
they are two years old.

What dangers does a platypus face?

Floods are dangerous for platypuses. Although the entrances to their burrows are above the water level, they are not high enough to protect them from flooding. Many die during severe floods, but their numbers seem to recover after a few years.

The building of dams can produce a lack of water in some platypus habitats, but they seem to be able to adapt and overcome this problem by moving to deeper pools.

Platypuses are protected animals and shouldn't be disturbed. They panic and suffer terrible stress if they hear unusual or loud noises.

Rubbish, pesticides, chemicals and other waste products pollute their habitats and can destroy them.

Enemies

Platypuses have enemies which will eat them if they are caught. In northern areas, crocodiles find them very tasty and it is possible for large eels to also eat them. Eagles take them and snakes will try to snatch them from their burrows. In southern areas, they can provide a source of food for the large Murray codfish. Feral foxes will also take them if they can.

What can people do to help?

- If you see a platypus in the wild, try to keep still and very quiet.
- If you see them in a zoo or sanctuary, keep very quiet and don't take photos.
- Flash light will frighten them. It is better to buy a photo at the gift shop.
- Pick up string, wire or plastic near waterways.
- If you are fishing and your line breaks, get it back.
- Don't throw rubbish in the water.
- Be careful when using poison and insecticides near waterways.
- Keep waterways clean of detergents, oil, metal, fish hooks, and drink cans.
- Encourage friends to adopt wildlife friendly strategies.

Platypuses can be seen in their natural habitat along the eastern side of Australia. They can also be seen in many zoos and sanctuaries. Here are some of them:

- Brisbane Forest Park Visitors Centre
- Fleay's Wildlife Centre, Burleigh Heads, Gold Coast
- Taronga Park Zoo, Sydney
- Warrawong Sanctuary, Mylor, South Australia
- Healesville Sanctuary, Victoria
- Kangaroo Island (in the wild)

Further reading:
Paradoxical Platypus, David Fleay, Jacaranda, QLD, 1980
The Platypus: A Unique Mammal, Tom Grant, NSW University Press, 1989

Web sites:
The University of Tasmania's monotreme site
www.healthsci.utas.edu.au/physiol/mono/Mainpage.html

Tropical Platypus Research
www.ozemail.com.au/~wildscap/platypusresearch.html

Wildlife Information and Rescue Services
www.streetnet.com.au/wires/3142.htm